The Psalm 37

MENAGERIE

Jeff Reed

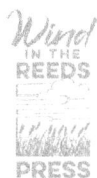

Wind
IN THE
REEDS

PRESS

172 Calvin Road
Cinebar, WA 98533

Wind in the Reeds

P R E S S

Wind in the Reeds Press, LLC
172 Calvin Road
Cinebar, WA 98533
www.windinthereedspress.com
windinthereedspub@gmail.com

Copyright 2023 by Jeff Reed
www.windinthereeds.com
Published 2023 by Wind in the Reeds Press

Cover Art original watercolor by Randi Lynn Reed
Used by permission
Visit her website at www.randilynnreed.com

Font: Palatino Linotype

10. 9. 8. 7. 6. 5.

ISBN – 978-1-7349176-8-0

Fret not yourself because of evildoers;
be not envious of wrongdoers!

⊕

I wake restless with
an unsatisfied sense
staring at the house
across the fence
and spot a
yellowjacket cone
tucked in the eaves,
busy about
the golden warriors
flying in and out
of their dimpled
waffle-paper home.
Suddenly I desire
one of my own.

For they will soon fade like the grass
and wither like the green herb.

⊕

I found the tangerine that had slid
some months ago behind the fridge
withered like a wrinkled walnut,
a sad dark globe which had upon it
continents of green-white mold,
a runaway planet, lifeless, cold.

iii

Trust in the Lord, and do good;
dwell in the land and cultivate faithfulness.

✠

From among the shards of glass
she picked up the intact flower pot,
its compact soil safe within,
and placed it on the splintered sill
(where the kitchen window had been
before the Russian missile blast
destroyed the school across the street)
and on it dribbled water from
her butterfly mug
with which she'd scooped
a little bit from underneath
the thin skin of wrinkled ice
fragile atop the rationed store of
what little was left in her bathroom tub.

iv

Delight yourself in the Lord,
and he will give you the desires of your heart.

☩

A man in the desert
without provision
merciless sun
endless terrain
all his desires
collapsed into one
stumbles upon
a shaded ravine
hearing within it
a trickling stream
the cold to his lips
the rushing relief

v

Commit your way to the Lord;
trust in him, and he will act.

⊕

I tried to put my thoughts in order—
a flock of sheep, far from the stall,
scattered on the pastured hillside,
unresponsive to my call.
My Aussie bolted at my bidding
the moment that I grabbed my pen.
Setting it to paper— how
the whole herd quietly filed in.

vi

He will bring forth your righteousness as the light,
and your justice as the noonday.

☩

Haman hated Mordecai —
smug beggar who refused to bow.
Sometimes in the morning I
see the silhouette of gallows
built for me. But here's the thing:
it is God Who will arrange the strange
road with twists so shrewd as to bring
forth who lives and who hangs.

Be still before the Lord and wait patiently for him;
fret not yourself over the one who prospers in his way,
over the man who carries out evil devices!

⊕

My hope rises
with every headlight
breaching the horizon
and falls as fast again
with every morphing form a car.
The posted schedule
helps me trust the bus
cannot be very far
and must have valid reasons
for it being late,
none to which I'm privy
as I shift my weight
and wait.

viii

Refrain from anger, and forsake wrath!
  Fret not yourself; it tends only to evil.

⊕

The white wolf
has worn away
the grass behind
her prison fence
with a plodding
back and forth
that never ceases.
At feeding time
the keeper throws
her meat. Before
she eats she tears
the chunks to pieces.

ix

For the evildoers shall be cut off,
but those who wait for the Lord shall inherit the land.

⊕

My friends went in
after an hour
to escape the cold,
disappointed in
the meteor shower
no show. Huddled
in my old sleeping bag,
I stayed to fill
the empty space
of night with hopeful
eyes until the skies
exploded with
a Perseids storm!
Underneath it
I was warm in wonder
and alone to see it.

In just a little while, the wicked will be no more;
though you look carefully at his place, he will not be there.

⊕

I spied the wasp nest
at the end of October
nestled into the
crook of an alder
crowded with lichens–
a mummified head
shrouded in silence,
nothing moving
in the failing twilight
over the ghost-house,
save a tremor of leaves
and memories of war,
the terrorist attacks
from the summer before.

But the humble shall inherit the land
and delight themselves in abundant peace.

⊕

Majestic cedar,
tower of green,
shading the palace
mezzanine,
adorned around
with lights on a string,
the plaque beneath it:
Tree of the King.

On the lip of a cliff
near the summit with neither
flora nor fauna
stands one scraggly cedar
whose crown touches clouds
whose view reaches seas,
who laughs through storms,
king of the trees.

The wicked plots against the righteous
and gnashes his teeth at him,

⊕

His *sorry* seems genuine–
 familiar refrain that spins
you in circles: making love
to violent shove and vicious
squeeze, me hiding bruises
beneath my sleeves. And
now this note of apology, an
ink-cloud perfect to screen
the hiding octopus waiting
 to grab from his camouflaged
lair some hapless crab.

xiii

but the Lord laughs at the wicked,
  for he sees that his day is coming.

✠

Plenty of laughter
going around:
grasshopper at the
leaf on the ground,
meerkat at the
hopper's brisk rub,
hyena at the mongoose
black-eyed mug,
lion laughing
at the laughing pack,
behind him the hunter,
a gun on his back,
mounting his trophy
head high on the wall,
down from heaven,
the loudest laugh of all.

xiv

The wicked draw the sword and bend their bows
to bring down the poor and needy,
to slay those whose way is upright;

⊕

From one tree,
from one good flitch
of wood laid
on the artisan's bench,
comes the riser
and limbs of the bow,
comes a dozen
shafts of perfect arrows,
comes the target with
fresh painted rings:
kin estranged
from each other on
the archery range.

Their sword shall enter their own heart,
and their bows shall be broken.

⊕

The spilt brown sugar
went everywhere.
It took an hour
to sweep it up,
the plastic dustpan
mounded high.
She tossed it out
the open door
into a gust
of wind that caught
the cloud and flung it
back inside.

*Better is the little that the righteous has
than the abundance of many wicked.*

⊕

The thief's pockets were
packed with plunder
from a busy night
on the Lido Deck:
diamond bracelets,
strings of pearl,
rare coins swept up
in the theft.
Within the hour
a freak reef strike
quickly brought
the old ship down.
Of all the passengers
floundering about,
only one of them
was drowned.

For the arms of the wicked shall be broken,
but the Lord sustains the righteous.

⊕

The Dark-eyed Junco
sits serenely on
the leafless branch,
swaying in cold drizzle,
looking this way,
then that, over winter's
haggard handiwork.

A sudden wind gust
rustles the dead
leaves piled
up against the
chain link fence,

while she perches
undisturbed
at this dull sheen
of scarcity–
vain veneer
over today's
as yet unseen
sustenance.

The Lord knows the days of the blameless,
and their heritage will remain forever.

⊕

On this moonless night
the forest floor is alive
with covert ops:
skittish rabbit hops,
voles emerging
from the ground,
tight-wound frogs,
timid field mice
scurrying around.
High above on
a granite crag,
the Great Horned Owl
sits like a king,
his keen eyes
and swiveling head
watching everything.

They are not put to shame in evil times;
in the days of famine they have abundance.

⊕

In Kerith ravine
cooled by shade
Elijah went hiding
to ride out the famine.
God sent ravens
to come to his aid
with a daily ration,
these creatures who
neither sow nor reap
bearing gifts of
bread and meat,
and this with water
from the trickling brook,
morning and evening,
and it was good.

xx

But the wicked will perish;
the enemies of the Lord are like the glory of the pastures;
they vanish—like smoke they vanish away.

⊕

We sat together
in the hot afternoon.
I felt a trickle of sweat
tickle as she pulled out
another cigarette.

I watched each
exhale-plume rise
like a writhing flower,
eager to bloom but
finding itself in
the air ill at ease,
expanding in search
of room to breathe,
vanishing into the
next wisp of breeze.

xxi

The wicked borrows but does not pay back,
but the righteous is generous and gives;

⊕

See the mountains
give their wealth away!
Selfless snowbanks
empty into rivers
splashing green on
woodland brown,
song over pebble
and frolicking fawn,
down to thirsty
furrowed farmland,
through the gluttonous
ungrateful city,
down, down
to the salty sea,
virtuous water
paying back her
mother's generosity.

xxii

For those blessed by the Lord shall inherit the land,
but those cursed by him shall be cut off.

⊕

This little wooded lot
holds a spell over me.
Old alder shade
on a hot afternoon
dapples the playful
stream teasing tips of
unraveled fern fronds
nodding up and down,
I along with them,
lulled into wonder
by the sound of
mockingbird songs
and wind in the firs.
I sit within sight of
 such remarkable works:
what nests, what webs,
what mole excavations!
What a beaver dam masterpiece:
its stripped sticks stitched
together so ingeniously–
just as I am to this
land and it to me.

The steps of a man are established by the Lord,
and He delights in his way;

⊕»

All around were arms outstretched:
protective mommy's in release,
daddy's waiting to receive,
baby's eagle-spread for balance
lurching over the carpet ocean,
toy boat tossed by unseen waves,
actor-captured staggering drunk
by the improvising year-old boy
tacking toward the harbor-father's
cheering voice's tremulous joy.

xxiv

Though he fall, he shall not be cast headlong,
for the Lord upholds his hand.

⊕

In the terrifying
nothingness
of the vacuum,
a brittle autumn leaf
falls as fast
as a heavy stone,
the shattering impact
fatal.

But break the seal,
let the *world-mothering*
air congeal,
and see that same leaf
float slowly down,
rocking back and forth
as gently as a
baby in a cradle.

xxv

I have been young, and now am old,
yet I have not seen the righteous forsaken
or his children begging for bread.

⊕

Three weeks ago
on a camping trip
we lost our dog Otto
in a freak thunderstorm.
The exhaustive search
that followed failed.

We awoke last night
to a familiar sound,
cheerful ring of a collar jingle.
We opened the door
to eager scratching,
and there sat Otto,
wagging his tail.

xxvi

He is ever lending generously,
and his children become a blessing.

☦

Among our company no leader
had brought a match or gas or lighter.
But one odd duck had flint and steel,

who rained down a spiel of sparks on a
tinder nest, nursing its flicker into
the best grade of dancing flame,

about which we gathered, young and old,
to warm our hands in the cold night air,
where even the shyest of us,

mesmerized by crackle and hiss,
joined in on wistful story-telling.
Just how many slipped out of the dark

with kindling to play Prometheus
I cannot say, but soon the whole beach
was a virtual fire-feast from the titans
down to the least of us.

xxvii

Turn away from evil and do good;
so shall you dwell forever.

⊕

After the wolf had blown
down the house of straw
and eaten bacon for breakfast,
he saw another house built
with thick sticks, the freshest
picks from winter's deadfall.
He blew that down too with
breath all the more bully, tough
lung punch breaking though.
He ate pig two for lunch,
after which he spied a house
made of bricks fresh-fired in
the local kiln. Confident from
recent success, he blew and blew
with visions of juicy pork-chops for
dinner. By midnight the moon
declared the mason pig the winner.

xxviii

For the Lord loves justice;
he will not forsake his saints.
They are preserved forever,
but the children of the wicked shall be cut off.

⊕

I don't know your name,
or how far away
in the world you are,
but you have something
that belongs to me,
treasure of your cruelty,
measure of my loss.
The cost as I try
to forgive is high,
but still I am sure
one day I will.
But even when I do,
know this to be true:
as long as you
hold illicit things
and do your best to hide it,
God's exquisite eyesight sees
your stash and does not like it.

xxix

*The righteous shall inherit the land
and dwell upon it forever.*

⊕

Around the time
of the Giza pyramids
a bristlecone pine
was finding its footing
on the high climes
of the eastern Sierras,
setting its sights
on living forever,
its resin-packed dense wood
impervious to pest
and adverse weather.
Having survived
the millenia test
without ostentation,
it may well yet
achieve its desire
and pass through fire
to the new creation.

xxx

The mouth of the righteous utters wisdom,
and his tongue speaks justice.

✠

Tina stopped after one mug of beer.
The other three continued chugging
prodigally well into the new year.
At closing time she confiscated
their keys without asking permission,
without saying please, articulating with
conviction: "I will drive and I alone."
After muddled protestations,
four women left the bar alive,
and alive four made it home.

xxxi

The law of his God is in his heart;
his steps do not slip.

✛

After replacing the
carpet with wood
the stairs were as glossy
 as a roller rink,
as slick as the porcelain
of a kitchen sink.
Descending in socks
was an auto-death wish.
Even Sunday's best lacked grip.
But court shoes and hi-tops
and rubber-bottomed slippers
wore the magic of spiders
and creepers and lizards,
were the wheels of a car
on a hill with new brakes.
O the difference
that a good sole makes.

xxxii

*The wicked spies upon the righteous
and seeks to kill him.*

✛

The hunter sits immobile in his blind,
alert eyes behind camouflage paint,
arrow notched in his Matthews bow,
waiting for deer to appear below.
The gray of early morning
passes into crisper light.
Alert for a whisper of a warning,
he shifts neither left nor right
in spite of screaming muscles,
staying perfectly still,
paying the price for the pleasure to kill.

xxxiii

The Lord will not abandon him to his power
or let him be condemned when he is brought to trial.

⊕

Invading microbes
in stealth mode
spread out
in a takeover bid
to destabilize
the health grid.
Helper T cells intercept,
and send out a Cytokine S.O.S.
A microphage calvary
descends upon
the germ soldiers,
swallowing them into
lysosome bellies,
spitting out
the acid remains.
B Cells alongside
memorize faces
as the evil company
steadily degrades,
efficiently finishing
the rescue job with
handy antibody grenades.

xxxiv

Wait for the Lord and keep his way,
and he will exalt you to inherit the land;
you will look on when the wicked are cut off.

⊕

Come, sunrise, again tomorrow.
Tide, your circadian blanket throw!
Leaves, return this Spring, outgrow
the gray of winter sorrow.
Shuffle through your phases, moon,
another cycle, another tide,
another dawn coaxing bright
diurnal birdsong into bloom.

xxxv

I have seen a wicked, ruthless man,
spreading himself like a green laurel tree.

⊕

The Himalayan Blackberry vines
have overwhelmed the alder like
a pride of lions gang-tackling wildebeest,
like sugar ants swarming an abandoned
piece of a piece of apple pie left
behind under the table.

The daggered tentacles, able to force
branches down toward the ground,
alter their lifetime trajectories,
showcasing in the years to visit
the bullies' power to do as they please
and get away with it.

xxxvi

But he passed away, and behold, he was no more;
though I sought him, he could not be found.

⊕

The Thanksgiving feast
was days in the making:
dreaming, planning,
shopping, sorting,
chopping, grating,
pulling out the finest china,
washing glasses, special sauces
marinating, kneading, baking,
choosing seating,
tasting, basting,
pasting, calling
all to come to
the sumptuous meal
with all the arduous
detailed preparation
finally finished!

(Every bit of it disappeared
in less than twenty minutes.)

xxxvii

Mark the blameless and behold the upright,
 for there is a posterity for the man of peace.

✠

I can't remember there
being so many foxgloves here.

Every year more and
more appear, it seems.

The corner lot, shorn of its trees,
has exploded into a color cacophony

from foxglove seeds long dormant
under the once shaded canopy.

I wonder where the first stalk
staked its belfry claim,

its lonely seeds catching wind
at the violent shaking

of a summer storm or playful deer–
ancestor of all the foxgloves flourishing here.

xxxviii

But transgressors shall be altogether destroyed;
the future of the wicked shall be cut off.

✛

Ripping up the third
overdue notice, he took a long shower,
and went about the rest of his day
without giving it a second thought,

until, having grown thirsty
in the middle of night,
the kitchen faucet mocked
his wanton disregard
by yielding nary a drop.

xxxix

The salvation of the righteous is from the Lord;
he is their stronghold in the time of trouble.

⊕

When the rapacious river,
roiling brown and angry,
left its banks to hunt down houses,
drown the innocent countryside
and everything living in it,
the ninety concrete pylons
holding up my home
appeared as unconcerned as if
the day instead was setting up
perfectly for a picnic.

xl

The Lord helps them and delivers them;
he delivers them from the wicked and saves them,
because they take refuge in him.

⊕

The sky is falling,
horizon on fire,
all that can be shaken
is rattling at a higher frenzy
since these forty days began–
span of the rainfall
over the floating menagerie,
of the desert waiting
with the wild beasts,
of the unknown fate
on the terrible mountain.
When Lent has spent
its seeping sorrow and I
am lost with help long overdue,
I calm myself and
once again choose You.

www.ingramcontent.com/pod-product-compliance
Lightning Source LLC
Chambersburg PA
CBHW032115040426
42337CB00041B/1349